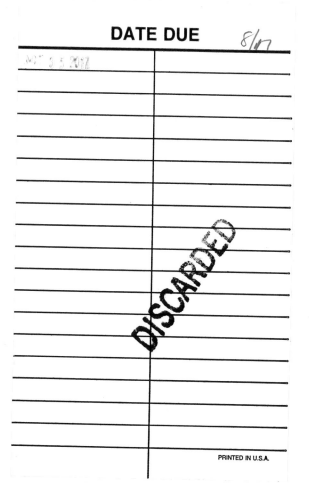

DATE DUE          8/17

| | |
|---|---|
| OCT 0 5 2012 | |
| | |
| | |
| | |
| | |
| | |
| | |
| | |
| | |
| | |
| | |
| | |
| | |
| | |
| | |
| | |
| | |
| | |
| | PRINTED IN U.S.A. |

# COOL CAREERS WITHOUT COLLEGE
# FOR PEOPLE WHO LOVE
# SHOPPING

REBECCA PELOS AND EDSON SANTOS

Rosen
YA
New York

*To Ane*

Published in 2018 by The Rosen Publishing Group, Inc.
29 East 21st Street, New York, NY 10010

**Library of Congress Cataloging-in-Publication Data**

Names: Pelos, Rebecca, author. | Santos, Edson, author.
Title: Cool careers without college for people who love shopping / Rebecca Pelos and Edson Santos.
Description: First edition. | New York, NY : Rosen Publishing Group, Inc., 2018. | Series: Cool careers without college | Audience: Grades 7–12 | Includes bibliographical references and index.
Identifiers: LCCN 2016059492 | ISBN 9781508175445 (library bound)
Subjects: LCSH: Purchasing—Vocational guidance—Juvenile literature. | Purchasing agents—Juvenile literature.
Classification: LCC HF5437 .S26 2018 | DDC 658.7023—dc23
LC record available at https://lccn.loc.gov/2016059492

*Manufactured in China*

# CONTENTS

# INTRODUCTION

For you, shopping might be a good form of stress relief. Or maybe you just really love looking for a bargain or filling a need in your life (or your wardrobe!) But shopping can be a lot more than a form of therapy, a pastime, a chore, or an obsession. With some fine-tuning, it can also be a pretty good way to make a living.

First, ask yourself what you enjoy buying. Do you find yourself looking up real estate listings online when you're bored? Do the holidays fill you with joy because they mean a trip to your favorite stores? Does the garage sale at the end of your block keep calling your name? Do you spend hours on eBay every day, looking for the one thing you're missing from your collection? The good news is that the skills it takes to make those purchases are all skills that can take you

Shopping provides many people with a great deal of enjoyment. Finding a bargain on a pair of shoes or a hard-to-find purse can fill a weekend or provide the perfect holiday gift.

forward into a career. Making purchases intelligently, for the best price, requires expertise—a lot of which you can gain without even planning for college. You can make a good living buying clothes, stocks, antiques, and even houses. All it takes is research, communication, negotiation skills, and networking with the right clients and suppliers. You can work for a large company or a small one or even start your own business. The business of buying and selling is filled with possibilities.

In the following sections, you'll learn about twelve different career paths for shopping enthusiasts. They cover a wide variety of interests to allow you to decide where you would like to go in your career. There are some occupations you might be considering already, and others that have not yet crossed your mind. Each section contains organizations, books, websites, and other helpful resources to help you figure out where you want to go next!

# CHAPTER 1

# PERSONAL SHOPPING ASSISTANT

Some people enjoy going to the store and trying on clothes or searching for other items. Other people dread the entire experience and feel stressed at the very mention of an event where a special outfit or gift is required. Do you know people who can't stand birthdays and holidays because it means spending hours searching for gifts that they know will just end up being exchanged? All of these problems are so common that they have led to the creation of a new profession: personal shopping. If you have a knack for shopping, you might make a great personal shopping assistant.

## WHAT THEY DO

Personal shopping assistants make purchases for people who 1) don't enjoy the shopping experience 2) do not have the time to shop for themselves or 3) have the personal and financial resources to hire someone to take care of purchases. Many personal shoppers specialize in shopping for clothing and accessories. Their clients are usually people with high profile jobs—artists, media figures, business people, and politicians—who are seen and judged by the public. Based on their body types, personalities, jobs, and lifestyles, you'll first help your clients discover what kind of styles and colors suit them. This involves knowing a good deal about fashion as well as different professions and social occasions (the proper attire for a lawyer is different from that of a rock star, best-selling author, or ambassador). You'll also need to understand people, their needs, insecurities, and sensitivities. Patience and tact are essential for a personal shopper.

Most personal shoppers are freelancers who work with clients on an individual basis. Some jobs might be one-time

Personal shoppers often use a smartphone to take pictures of potential purchases and to keep in touch with clients.

projects. For instance, a television journalist wants to change her image and update her wardrobe. You might begin with a consultation at her home where you both go through her wardrobe and decide which clothes look good on her and which don't. Some articles can be given away and donated, while others might be altered. Then, based on your client's measurements, needs, and budget, you'll go on a shopping spree. It helps to have good personal relationships with designers and retailers at department stores and boutiques. Often, you can work out an agreement whereby you can return or exchange clothes that don't fit or suit your client. Sometimes, you can even get discounts.

After bringing your finds to your client, you will both "edit" the new wardrobe, deciding what to keep, what to return, and what needs tailoring. Some shoppers help accessorize clothing with jewelry, shoes, and bags and work with clients on how to create different looks by mixing pieces. Making someone look and feel good about him- or herself can be very gratifying. If pleased with your work, some people might become permanent clients. They'll call you if they need a special outfit for an awards ceremony, some suits for a business trip, or even back-to-school clothes for their kids. Some people even seek out shoppers for advice on what to wear at a criminal court trial or when getting a divorce.

# A TALE OF TWO PERSONAL SHOPPERS

Mary Walbridge is a costume designer working in the film and television industries in Los Angeles. She has been nominated for two Emmy awards for her work as a costume supervisor for the television show Will & Grace. Mary is also a stylist and personal shopper who has shopped for celebrities such as Matt Damon, Michael Douglas, Demi Moore, and Glenn Close. Aside from general shopping services, Mary offers shopping services for bridal and holiday parties, black tie events, and career changes. Per hour, she charges $250 for a consultation, $150 for cleaning out closets, and $100 for shopping. Shoppers with experience and clients such as Mary's can make around $100,000 a year.

Laurie Ely of Chicago stumbled onto personal shopping by accident. When she bought groceries at her local supermarket, Laurie was often approached by elderly people who couldn't read labels or reach items on high shelves. Divorced and with three children to feed, Laurie printed up flyers announcing the services of "Laurie the Shopping Lady," which she posted around her neighborhood. Before long, she had such a long client list that grocery shopping came to mean pushing five carts full of groceries and spending over $100,000 a year. By charging 15 percent commission plus an $8 shopping fee, she earns over $20,000 a year as well as the appreciation of many lonely retirees.

Some personal shoppers shop for items other than clothes. For many people, purchasing presents—particularly around the holidays when stores are packed and shopping lists seem endless—can be stressful and time consuming. Many corporations also rely on personal shoppers when they need to buy gifts for clients, suppliers, and employees.

Although most personal shoppers have their own businesses, some work for shopping malls or large department stores such as Macy's, Bergdorf Goodman, and Neiman Marcus, all of whom offer personal shopping services. Customers who want wardrobe advice and individual attention—and often access to private fitting rooms—rely on these personal shoppers. They often receive a commission or a shopper's fee along with their salary.

## PREPARING FOR A CAREER AS A PERSONAL SHOPPER

Good personal shoppers know everything there is to know about the latest fashion and new products. Reading books and staying up-to-date with trends via magazines and style reports is essential. So is hitting shops and talking to retailers. You'll need to be aware of what is available (and for how much) from sources as diverse as major department stores, vintage boutiques, sample sales, new designer fairs, and

A good personal shopper keeps up on the latest fashion trends, reading fashion magazines and even attending fashion shows.

websites. Some professional shoppers offer seminars and courses for people who want to get into the field.

The best way to gain knowledge and work experience is to get a part-time job in retail sales. Working weekends in a local boutique gives you insight into customers' personalities and shopping patterns, which allows you to hone your advising skills. In the meantime, offer your shopping services to friends and family members.

# JOB OUTLOOK AND SALARY

Based on the amount of projects available and clients' budgets, salaries for professional shoppers vary enormously. According to Glassdoor.com, the average personal shopper makes around $27,000 per year, but personal shoppers employed by chains like Macy's might earn at least $48,000, depending on experience.

To date, the professional shopping field is quite small. This means that while there is a lot of competition, there is great opportunity for enterprising shoppers. People who need individual attention in a society where time is increasingly precious will continue to benefit from the services of personal shoppers.

# FOR MORE INFORMATION

## ORGANIZATIONS

Association of Image Consultants International
1000 Westgate Drive, Suite 252
St. Paul, MN 55114
(651) 290-7468
Website: http://www.aici.org/
With local chapters throughout Canada and the
United States, this organization promotes image
consulting as a profession and provides education,
training, job resources, and reports on new trends
and fashions to those who work in the field, including
personal shoppers.

## BOOKS

Halbreich, Betty. *I'll Drink to That: New York's Legendary
Personal Shopper and Her Life in Style - With a Twist.*
London, UK: Virago, 2014.

## PERIODICALS

*Domino Magazine*
Condé Nast Publications
4 Times Square, 17th Floor

New York, NY 10036
Website: http://www.dominomag.com/
This print magazine describes itself as a personal
shopper. Specializing in items for the home in a
variety of styles and price ranges, it also features
exclusive giveaways and discounts.

Lucky Magazine
Condé Nast Publications
4 Times Square, 17th Floor
New York, NY 10036
Website: http://www.luckymag.com
A shopping magazine that helps you track down
anything you might desire, from clothing and
cosmetics to housewares and furnishings.

## WEBSITES

Because of the changing nature of internet links, Rosen
Publishing has developed an online list of websites
related to the subject of this book. This site is updated
regularly. Please use this link to access the list:

http://www.rosenlinks.com/CCWC/shopping

# CHAPTER 2

## RETAIL BUYER

Have you ever dreamed of spending hundreds of thousands of dollars on something and then being paid for it? Not for yourself, of course, but for the owners of a retail store. Imagine purchasing hundreds of toys, thousands of chocolate bars, or a few dozen designer dresses that you glimpsed upon the fashion runways of New York, Paris, and Milan. If you find the notion appealing, consider that such buying sprees are a major part of the job of a retail buyer.

Retail buyers often meet with designers to decide whether or not to stock a certain item or line of items in a store.

# WHAT THEY DO

Retail buyers select and purchase merchandise for stores and companies. These companies might be large and run chain stores such as CVS and Macy's, and discount stores like Target and Wal-Mart. Other companies might be small, like clothing boutiques. Some buyers also purchase goods and products that are sold through catalogs or over the Internet. In general, buyers specialize in a specific type of product, such as men's shoes, children's books, or silverware. Often, the larger the store, the more specialized the buyers.

As a large-scale retail buyer, you won't usually go out shopping for products. In most cases you'll work at the main business office of your store or company. Buyers for small stores often work in the store itself. If you're purchasing manufactured goods such as clothing, furniture, appliances, toys, cosmetics, or packaged goods, you'll often order them directly from the manufacturer. You'll probably buy other products such as clothing, accessories, fresh fish, meat, fruit, vegetables, plants, and flowers from wholesalers. Wholesalers buy goods from many different individual suppliers, such as farms or craftspeople, and resell them to retail buyers in large quantities.

Retail buyers don't simply decide what to buy based on their own tastes. Careful research must be done about what the buying public, and specifically the public that shops in your store, wants. Aside from knowing who your customers are and what kind of tastes and budgets they have, you also have to be aware of market trends, new products, and the state of the general economy—factors that can change daily. A lot can be learned from visiting trade fairs and suppliers, reading trade journals, and also checking out the competition. Buyers spend considerable time shopping around for products to see which manu-facturers or wholesalers offer the best prices, quality, and variety. Some buyers, especially fashion buyers who must stay up on the latest runway trends, even travel abroad.

Forging close relationships with suppliers is another important part of a buyer's job. You'll need to negotiate good prices with suppliers and make sure they can deliver on time. Deciding what items shoppers will want, how many to buy, and at what price they can be sold can be exciting but stressful. If your estimates are wrong, the store will be left with a surplus of unsold merchandise. The store will lose money and you'll be largely to blame. If, however, customers buy the items you choose, the store, or at least your depart-ment, will make profits.

# THE LIFE OF A CANDY BUYER

While retail buyers usually don't start out with a specialization, they often end up with one. Depending on their interests and the needs of the employer, they often end up focusing on a specific area. Take Valeria Stansfield, for example. She specializes in candy. In fact, she buys candy and snacks for the Rite Aid chain of drug stores in the United States. Valeria's purchasing decisions have an impact on the candy that is sold in more than 3,600 stores in over thirty states. Ironically, when Valeria was a student she had hopes of becoming a dentist. Instead she began her retail career as a buyer of children's clothing and then switched to another popular children's item—and a dentist's worst enemy—candy.

Valeria credits her success as a buyer to several factors. She is always willing to try new products, providing the manufacturers can prove why their goods are so great. She also stays attuned to the different tastes and buying patterns in various markets. For example, she has discovered that the candy people eat on the East Coast is very different from what people on the West Coast like. Consequently, she buys different product mixes for stores in different regions. Last, but not least, she loves candy! There isn't any candy being sold in any of the 3,600 drug stores she buys for that she hasn't sucked, crunched, or bitten into herself.

# PREPARING FOR A CAREER

Because of the competitive market, many businesses require that retail buyers have a BA in business or marketing, or some related courses at a community college. However, many stores and companies, particularly smaller ones, favor employees who have worked their way up through various retail positions. In fact, many buyers start out working in stores where they gain retail experience and are then hired as assistant or junior buyers. A lot of major chain stores, such as Macy's and Wal-Mart, have their own in-house buyer training programs for employees. After training as an assistant or junior buyer, you can be promoted to an associate buyer, in charge of purchases for a specific section of a store. Over time, you can then become a full-fledged buyer who, aside from purchasing for an entire department, supervises associate buyers and interns. At the top of the purchasing pyramid are senior buyers and purchasing directors, whose function is to oversee all retail purchases for a store or company.

# JOB OUTLOOK AND SALARY

Buyers who are just starting out—assistant or junior buyers—can earn between $23,000 to $30,000 a year. Depending on the store and the length of time they've been working, associate buyers and full-fledged buyers might earn anywhere between $50,000 and $100,000 a year. Senior buyers for large retailers or department stores can earn $150,000 a year or more. Although earnings can be high, an average work week can often surpass forty hours, particularly around the holidays, when working late nights and weekends is common.

Of course, an added bonus is that you can usually get some good discounts on store merchandise!

Retail jobs in general are dependent on the state of the economy. When the economy is booming, consumers spend more and stores therefore need more buyers to

Working late nights can be common during busy times of the year. But long hours may be more manageable if you communicate your needs to your manager.

purchase merchandise. In a poor economy, retailers tend to cut back on employees. With regard to the long-term future, opportunities for retail buyers will probably become more scarce. As big chains expand and replace smaller, independent stores, fewer buyers are responsible for a larger number of stores. Meanwhile, computers and technology are able to perform and simplify many tasks—such as accounting, ordering, tracking shipments, and maintaining inventory—that were formerly done by buyers. As a result, a single buyer can do the work previously done by two or three people.

# FOR MORE INFORMATION

## ORGANIZATIONS

National Retail Federation
1101 New York Avenue NW
Washington, DC 20005
(800) NRF-HOW2 or (202) 783-7971
Website: http://www.nrf.com
The world's largest retail trade association represents
an industry with more than 1.4 million U.S. retail
establishments and more than 23 million employees.

Retail Council of Canada
1881 Yonge Street, Suite 800
Toronto, ON M4S 3C4
Canada
(416) 467-3777
Website: http://www.retailcouncil.org/
The voice of Canadian retail, RCC represents
department stores, mass merchants, specialty chains,
and independent and online stores throughout
Canada. Its website lists industry news and
information about events, education, and resources.

## BOOKS

Friedman, Harry J. *No Thanks, I'm Just Looking: Sales Techniques for Turning Shoppers into Buyers*. Hoboken, NJ: Wiley, 2012.

Ramsey, Dan and Judy Ramsey. *The Everything Guide to Starting and Running a Retail Store: All You Need to Get Started and Succeed in Your Own Retail Adventure*. Avon, MA: Adams Media, 2010.

*Start Your Own Clothing Store and More: Women's, Men's, Children's, Speciality*. Irvine, CA: Entrepreneur Press, 2011.

## WEBSITES

Because of the changing nature of internet links, Rosen Publishing has developed an online list of websites related to the subject of this book. This site is updated regularly. Please use this link to access the list:

http://www.rosenlinks.com/CCWC/shopping

# CHAPTER 3

# INTERIOR DESIGNER/ DECORATOR

Do you enjoy spending time on Pinterest and other home design websites? Do you enjoy flipping through decorator magazines or housewares catalogs, imagining what would look good in the enormous rooms of your fantasy house? Chances are, in reality, your room is too small and your budget too tiny for the furniture and art you crave. However, as an interior decorator you can satisfy your yearnings and even make a decent living by buying furniture and decorative objects for other people who do have the space and the budget, but lack the time or inclination to decorate themselves.

The role of a decorator is to seek out quality pieces to bring "something special" to a room. This might be as large as a couch or as small as an accent pillow.

# WHAT THEY DO

Interior decorators decorate home interiors, offices, hotels, restaurants, bars, and boutiques. As a decorator you'll rely on your natural flair, eye for detail, sense of color, and experience to decide how to make a space both functional and beautiful. You'll need to be good at making decisions such as what color carpeting a hallway should have, what fabrics should be used for curtains, and what pieces of furniture work well together and how they should be arranged. At the same time, you'll have to know what furnishing resources and products exist and where to buy them. Tracking down a rare, eighteenth-century Portuguese antique chair for someone's home or an authentic stagecoach wheel as decoration for a Tex-Mex restaurant can be interesting challenges. It can also be a challenge to bargain for a price that will satisfy your client's budget. Just as important as building a list of faithful clients is establishing relationships with furniture manufacturers and retailers; antique stores; art galleries; paint, lighting and hardware stores; and housewares shops. Being on good terms with suppliers allows you to stay up-to-date about new products and obtain discounts on purchases.

Since your livelihood as a decorator depends on your clients, you must be sensitive to their needs. Some clients will depend on your advice. They may not be sure what they want or what decorative solutions are available for their budget.

Lighting can make or break a good room design. An inexpensive lamp can light a dark corner of a room or decorate an ordinary end table.

It is important to find solutions that are as economical and functional as they are beautiful.

Taking their desires into account, you'll develop one or more proposals for their approval. Your proposals will take into account space, lighting, color schemes, paint, fabrics, flooring, doors, and windows, and use of accessories such as rugs, pillows, art objects, and even plants. Once your plans have been approved, you'll go shopping for the agreed-upon furnishings and supplies. Your clients might also want you to

## DECORATING THROUGH THE YEARS

Betty Sherrill who passed away in 2014 at the age of ninety-one, spent years as the Chairwoman of McMillen, Inc., America's first professional, full-service interior design firm (founded in 1923). Betty worked for over fifty years at McMillen. Over the years, she decorated houses for Rockefellers, Kennedys, and the palace of a sheik from Kuwait. She even decorated the White House (when President Johnson and his family were living there).

Betty's first decorating job was the third floor of her family's house in New Orleans when she was still a girl. New wallpaper and a shocking shade of pink in the stairway were the results. In her youth, she also loved combing through antique shops. To those who want to enter the field of home decorating, she has suggested taking decorating courses at art or design school. She also has advised that while decorators should keep up with trends, they shouldn't always copy them. As a case in point, she didn't redecorate her own house for over forty years.

recommend painters, carpenters, and other tradespeople and oversee their work.

Many decorators are freelancers who have their own businesses. They get jobs from personal recommendations and aggressive marketing of their services via ads and websites. Others have full-time staff jobs with decorating or design firms.

Although decorating can be fun, it can also be stressful when the decorator is juggling more than one project. Trying to meet deadlines while dealing with unforeseen problems—from no—show workers to decorative "mistakes" such as mismatched colors and objects that don't work together and fussy clients—requires strong problem-solving skills and lots of patience.

## PREPARING FOR YOUR CAREER

Although no formal training or education is necessary to become an interior decorator, some knowledge of art is useful, as is math for doing measurements and calculations. Decorating courses are available at art schools, community colleges, and continuing education programs, but you can learn a lot just by consulting decorating and design books and magazines, visiting retailers, window shopping, and checking out interestingly furnished restaurants and hotels. Start downloading or clipping out photographs of design objects and decorator solutions that you admire and build up your own personal archive of material. Check out Pinterest and other online resources for design ideas.

Once you've decorated and redecorated your own room, see if your parents, neighbors, or family friends will let you tackle theirs. Make sure to take before and after photographs of your work for a portfolio that you can show future clients.

Another good way to learn about decorating and make contacts is to get a part-time job at a decorating firm or retail store specializing in furniture, design objects, and home furnishings.

## JOB OUTLOOK AND SALARY

Based on experience and location, an interior decorator can make anywhere between $30,000 and $50,000 a year. Many decorators work out of their homes as part-time freelancers and don't depend exclusively on their decorators' earnings. An experienced decorator with formal training, a good reputation, and a list of important clients with large budgets can earn $100,000 or more. While some of these high-earning decorators own their own small companies, others work for design or decorating firms or furniture retailers that pay high salaries.

According to the U.S. Department of Labor, jobs for interior decorators should increase by more than 4 percent over the next few years. As people become more conscious of design, and as design solutions become increasingly accessible and affordable, both businesses and individuals are seeking out the professional help of decorators to create unique spaces. At the same time, the competitiveness of this field means that good jobs go to those with the most experience and education.

# FOR MORE INFORMATION

## ORGANIZATIONS

American Society of Interior Designers
1152 15th Street NW, Suite 910
Washington, DC 20005
(202)546-3480
Website: https://www.asid.org
The American Society of Interior Designers (ASID)
    is a community of people—designers, industry
    representatives, educators and students—committed
    to interior design.

Canadian Decorators' Association (CDECA)
10 Morrow Avenue, Suite 202
Toronto, ON M6R 2J1
Canada
(888) 878-2155
Website: http://www.cdeca.com/
Information and resources for Canada's association of
    professional interior decorators and designers.

Certified Interior Decorators International (CID)
649 SE Central Parkway
Stuart, FL 34994

(772) 287-1855
Website: http://www.cidinternational.org/
An association, with education and certification
    programs, for professional decorators.

Interior Design Society
164 S. Main Street, Suite 404
High Point, NC 27260
(336) 884-4437
Website: http://www.interiordesignsociety.org/
The Interior Design Society (IDS) is one of the country's
    largest design organizations dedicated to serving the
    residential interior design industry. IDS embraces four
    core values including professionalism, community,
    influence and growth.

International Interior Design Association
222 Merchandise Mart, Suite 567
Chicago, IL 60654
(888) 799-4432
Website: http://www.iida.org
IIDA, with respect for past accomplishments of Interior
    Design leaders, strives to create a strong niche for

the most talented and visionary Interior Design professionals, to elevate the profession to the level it warrants, and to lead the way for the next generation of Interior Design innovators.

## BOOKS

Dellatore, Carl, editor. *Interior Design Master Class: 100 Lessons from America's Finest Designers on the Art of Decoration*. New York, NY: Rizzoli, 2016.

Henderson, Emily and Angelin Borsics. *Styled: Secrets for Arranging Rooms, from Tabletops to Bookshelves*. New York, NY: Potter Style, 2015.

Liess, Lauren. *Habitat: The Field Guide to Decorating*. New York, NY: Harry N. Abrams, 2015.

O'Shea, Linda, Chris Grimley, and Mimi Love. *The Interior Design Reference & Specification Book: Everything Interior Designers Need to Know Every Day*. Beverly, MA: Rockport Publishers, 2013.

## PERIODICALS

Elle Décor
Hachette Filipacchi Media

300 W. 57th Street, 28th floor
New York, NY 10019
Website: http://www.elledecor.com/
Stylish print magazine with beautiful photos and
    articles on home design and living.

## WEBSITES

Because of the changing nature of internet links, Rosen
Publishing has developed an online list of websites
related to the subject of this book. This site is updated
regularly. Please use this link to access the list:

http://www.rosenlinks.com/CCWC/shopping

# CHAPTER 4

# PROPS ASSISTANT

Working in the props department is a little bit like a treasure hunt. Do you like using clues to find a specific item and racing to find it before anybody else? You might be a great candidate to work as a props assistant or prop buyer. Prop buyers track down frequently hard-to-find, unusual objects to be used for films, plays, TV shows, advertisements, and magazine layouts. If the notion of hunting treasure for a living appeals to you, you might want to look into becoming a prop buyer.

## WHAT THEY DO

Props are used in movies, plays, and television. They decorate the set or are used by actors to help tell the story. A set of Victorian china, a potted orchid, a unicycle, a goldfish in a bowl, a cell phone, a gun—all of these are props. Depending on a director's needs and vision and the prop budget, props will either be constructed or purchased. In the latter case, the

Do you have what it takes to find the perfect, historically accurate lamp, doll, or concert poster?

prop manager, who oversees all props, will hire a prop buyer to track down and buy or rent the items needed.

Buying props often entails a great deal of research as well as a lot of footwork. Prop rental shops and websites (such as eBay) abound. Some specialize in exotic items such as medieval armor, monster and horror props, and even fake corpses outfitted with a variety of wounds and degrees of skin decay. Nonetheless, it's not always easy to unearth a pair of seventeenth-century dueling swords, a nineteenth-century baby carriage, or a boomerang. To find such things quickly and without paying a fortune, you'll have to be resourceful, imaginative, and quick-thinking. You'll also need to be very organized. You must be capable of sticking to a tight budget and keeping track of all expenses, including purchases and rentals, shipping and transportation, and cab fares. Also essential is comfortable footwear. (There is so much running around in this job that some prop buyers deduct foot massages as a business-related expense!)

Props are also widely used in television commercials; print advertisements; and photographic layouts for catalogs, magazines, and even packaging (who do you think found those plates and napkins for the photograph on the Lean Cuisine package?). In these cases, many prop buyers, also known as prop stylists, work with or are hired by photographers. When photographers are hired by the art director of a magazine, catalog, or ad agency to shoot a layout or campaign, they usually bring along a prop stylist whom they work with on a regular basis. As a stylist or shopper, you'll need to take orders from the art director and then go hunting for whatever he or she requires for a specific shoot. This often means interpreting what exactly you think the director wants, which can be a challenge. Sometimes your instructions may be vague, such as "Find me a scary-looking sculpture," or "Get me some Russian peasant lanterns." Other missions,

# THE LIFE OF A PROP STYLIST

Originally a fashion merchandiser at a Manhattan department store, Judy Singer has been making a living as an independent prop stylist in New York for close to three decades. She finds and purchases props that will surround products featured in print advertisements. Her specialty is "tabletop styling." Due to Singer's talent for tracking down the perfect pen for any desk or table, she and a photographer with whom she often works are known as the top ten photographer-stylist team in New York.

More often, however, Singer works with food. While the food stylist prepares the food, and a carpenter constructs a kitchen set, Singer consults with the art director before going off to purchases dishes, tablecloths, napkins, flowers, and any other objects needed to create the scene the art director wants. Sometimes interpreting a director's wishes is tricky. She recalls one director who told her he wanted a table out of an Italian movie, with an air of seduction, hand-made pottery, and "really masculine" cheese. Skilled at interpreting what directors want and always up on the latest trends and products, Singer usually shows up with a few potential options. She is present during the photo shoot in case any last-minute prop shopping is required. Having worked for clients ranging from General Electric and Nestlé to InStyle and Bon Appétit magazines, she says that it's important to put your own taste on hold in order to please your client.

such as discovering fresh blackberries in December, might seem next to impossible. Relying on your creativity and experience, you'll need to find one, or several options that the director can choose from.

## PREPARING FOR YOUR CAREER

Learning on the job is one of the best ways to gain experience as a prop buyer. In the world of film, television, and theater, many prop managers or buyers hire assistants to do jobs such as picking up, returning, organizing, and taking care of props. To learn about advertising and print work, assisting stylists, photographers, or art directors is a good introduction to the profession and an excellent way to make contacts. Since getting jobs in this field depends almost exclusively on

Theater, TV, and movie props can be almost anything. One day you might decorate an item with hundreds of feathers. The next, you might be repairing a lamp.

recommendations and personal references, it is good to make as many contacts as possible. Other related jobs that can be useful include working for a prop or costume rental company.

## JOB OUTLOOK AND SALARY

Prop buyers are often freelancers who work on short-term projects. While you're working, hours are often long and intense (fourteen-hour days with evening and weekend work are the norm). One week, you might have three assignments where you make $2,000 in three or four days. Then you might spend a month waiting nervously for the phone to ring. Top prop shoppers and stylists with a strong reputation and a list of important clients can earn $800 a day for advertising work and $400 to $500 a day for editorial work in magazines. Prop shoppers who work in film, television, and particularly in theater, earn less, sometimes averaging only between $25,000 and $35,000 a year.

Prop shopping is a fairly small field and is quite competitive. Many job opportunities tend to be in large cities where media, art, and publishing industries are located. The secret to success is building up a strong reputation and specializing in a certain type of prop or specific kind of client. Becoming a prop manager, designing and making props, or opening your own prop shop are other related occupations.

# FOR MORE INFORMATION

## ORGANIZATIONS

The Broadway League
729 Seventh Avenue, 5th floor
New York, NY 10019
(212) 764-1122
Website: https://www.broadwayleague.com/
The Broadway League is the national trade association
for the Broadway industry.

International Alliance of Theatrical Stage Employees
(IATSE)
207 W. 25th Street, 4th floor
New York, NY 10001
(212) 730-1770
Website: http://www.iatse.net/
IATSE is the main labor union representing technicians
and craftspeople in the entertainment industry,
including theater, film, and television.

The Shubert Organization
234 West 44th Street
New York, NY 10036
(212) 944-3700

Website: http://www.shubertorganization.com/
The Shubert Organization has been at the forefront of
   American theatre since the start of the 20th century.
   The company currently owns and operates seventeen
   Broadway theatres and six off-Broadway venues.

Theatre Association of New York State
PO Box 4143
Rome, NY 13442
Website: http://www.tanys.org/
TANYS combines the strengths of two organizations
   that have served nonprofessional theatre in New York
   State for a combined total of more than 70 years.

Theatre Communications Group
520 Eighth Ave., 24th floor
New York, NY 10018
(212) 609-5900
Website: https://www.tcg.org/
Theatre Communications Group (TCG), the national
   organization for the American theatre, was founded in
   1961 with a grant from the Ford Foundation to foster
   communication among professional, community and
   university theatres.

# BOOKS

Campbell, Drew. *Technical Theater for Nontechnical People*, 2nd ed. New York, NY: Allworth Press, 2012.

Hart, Eric. *The Prop Building Guidebook: For Theatre, Film, and TV*. Oxford, UK: Focal Press, 2013.

Strawn, Sandra. *The Properties Director's Handbook: Managing a Prop Shop for Theatre*. Oxford, UK: Focal Press, 2012.

Viertel, Jack. *The Secret Life of the American Musical: How Broadway Shows Are Built*. New York, NY: Sarah Crichton Books, 2016.

# PERIODICALS

Live Design
1166 Avenue of the Americas, 10th floor
New York, NY 10036
(212) 204-4272
Website: http://livedesignonline.com/
Industry news, features, and interviews with professionals involved in behind-the-scenes theater professions. The website includes links to industry resources.

The World of Interiors
Condé Nast U.K.
Vogue House, 1 Hanover Square
London W1S 1JU
United Kingdom
Website: http://www.worldofinteriors.co.uk/
Published in England, this influential and informative
    glossy magazine is considered one of the world's
    leading sources for stylists, designers, and interior
    decorators.

## WEBSITES

Because of the changing nature of internet links, Rosen
Publishing has developed an online list of websites
related to the subject of this book. This site is updated
regularly. Please use this link to access the list:

http://www.rosenlinks.com/CCWC/shopping

# CHAPTER 5

# REALTOR

Buying a new home is one of the most important decisions of a person's life. If they make a poor decision, buyers can end up losing money and being miserable. However, if they purchase wisely, they will end up with a valuable investment that will greatly enhance their lives. Often the person who makes the difference is a real estate agent. If you would enjoy the satisfaction of helping people find their ideal residential or commercial space and earning a substantial commission in the process, you might consider a career as a real estate agent.

## WHAT THEY DO

Realtors or real estate agents help people find and purchase homes and other property. To do this, they must first discover owners who want to sell property. While many sellers themselves contact real estate firms, agents also spend a lot of time on the phone trying to get listings. Knowing the market in your neighborhood and having many contacts

Real estate agents work one-on-one with clients to help them find homes and offices within a set budget and neighborhood.

who can give you tips about what might come up for sale are essential. The majority of real estate agents are involved in buying and selling residential properties. They usually start out by getting listings of properties for sale in their own communities or towns, either by word of mouth or by doing research. For example, families that have suffered deaths, divorces, or financial problems often need to sell their homes. Knowing the neighborhood is important, since homebuyers consider more than just a house or apartment in itself. Depending on their ages and interests, buyers are also influenced by factors such as security; noise; convenience; and proximity to public transportation, shopping areas, schools, and recreation areas such as parks and bike paths.

Most real estate agents are independent contractors who work for real estate broker. Some brokers are small firms with a few employees, while others are franchises of large national companies such as Royal LePage or Century 21. In return for finding properties and closing sales between buyers and sellers, the broker pays the agent part of the commission made from the sale. While agents spend a lot of time in the field, brokers manage the office, monitor agents, and tend to the business and administrative details of real estate transactions.

As an agent, you'll spend a lot of time making phone calls and keeping your eyes and ears open for people who have property to sell. Your goal is to get sellers to list their properties with you. When people want to buy a home, they'll contact you and ask to see your listings. After meeting with clients to determine what they're looking for and how much they can spend, you'll select promising properties from your list and set up a time to visit them with the clients. Often, visits will take place in the evening or on weekends, when your clients are available. Being sensitive to your clients' needs and what exactly they're looking for are key for a successful agent. And when buyers have questions—How old is the furnace? What are the local zoning laws? How much are property taxes? Is the property in a flood zone?—it is your job to find out the answers.

If the buyers are interested in a certain property, you want to do everything you can to help them obtain a good deal. If the asking price is steep, you can help negotiate with the seller or recommend banks and mortgage companies where the buyer can get financing. As an agent, you act as a mediator between buyers and sellers. Buyers might ask

Much of buying and selling a home involves a lot of paperwork, and a realtor will know every step of the process and every line that requires a signature.

you to negotiate certain renovations or recommend a house inspector to make sure the house is in good condition. Once both sides have agreed on a price and details of the transfer, the agent is responsible for drawing up a contract. When the contract has been signed and the sale finalized, everybody should end up a winner: buyers will have their new home, sellers will have their money, and you will have the satisfaction of a job well done along with your commission.

Some real estate agents buy and sell commercial property. Commercial property includes office and retail space, hotels and restaurants, factories, warehouses, and land to be developed, as well as industrial and agricultural real estate. Commercial real estate agents usually work for large or specialized companies and focus on one type of commercial real estate—office space, for example. It is essential to have a lot of knowledge concerning the type of property you are dealing with as well as the specific business needs of your clients. For instance, if you are selling a factory, you'll need to inform your buyer about factors such as the region's transportation systems, utilities, and labor supply.

## PREPARING FOR YOUR CAREER

The background that most real estate agents share is a high school diploma and solid communication skills. An increasing number of people, however, are taking real estate courses at community or junior colleges. Local associations affiliated with the National Association of Realtors also offer courses on various aspects of real estate. However, the best way to train for a real estate career is by acquiring on-the-job experience. Try to get an assistant's job or internship with a firm in your neighborhood. You'll usually start off helping agents or brokers by answering phones and trying to get property listings.

Before you can call yourself a real estate agent, you have to be eighteen years old and obtain a license. Each state and province has its own set of requirements, including practical experience, course work, and one or more exams. Often, larger brokers offer their own training sessions and preparatory classes.

## JOB OUTLOOK AND SALARY

Most real estate agents don't earn salaries, but commissions. Commissions are a percentage of the price buyers pay for property. The longer you work and the more successful you are, the higher the commissions you will make. Because they have no clients and little experience, agents who are starting out make almost no money in their first year. It could take weeks or months to get your first sale. Over time however, as your sales increase, you can make between $20,000 and

$50,000 a year. The top 10 percent of agents make over $105,000. It is the possibility of making such high earnings that motivates many agents.

As population and real estate development in North America continue to grow, people will be moving more and buying and selling more property. North Americans also increasingly view real estate as a sound financial investment. Many people buy homes or buildings that they then rent out, or renovate and resell for a profit. All of these factors will mean more opportunities for real estate agents. The spread of technology, however, will also allow a single agent to do the work formerly done by several. Instead of traveling to visit properties, agents and clients can view exteriors and interiors on the Internet. Cell phones and computers minimize the time spent on transactions and even allow many agents to work at home instead of at brokers' offices.

# FOR MORE INFORMATION

## ORGANIZATIONS

National Association of Exclusive Buyer Agents
1481 N. Eliseo Felix Way, #100
Avondale, AZ 85323
(623) 932-0098
Website: http://www.naeba.org/
Buyer agents work exclusively with buyers (instead
  of sellers) to help them locate, finance, inspect, and
  purchase the ideal property. This association's website
  offers lists of exclusive buyer agents.

National Association of Realtors
430 North Michigan Avenue
Chicago, IL 60611-4087
(800) 874-6500
Website: http://www.realtor.org
The United States' leading organization for realtors
  offers a wealth of information concerning every
  aspect of national and international real estate.

Real Estate Institute of Canada
5407 Eglinton Avenue West, Suite 208
Toronto, ON M9C 5K6
Canada

(416) 695-9000

Website: http://www.reic.ca

An association that educates and certifies Canadian real estate professionals and creates networking opportunities between agents and brokers.

## BOOKS

Doyle, Brandon, Nicholas Dreher, and Marshall Saunders. *Mindset, Methods & Metrics: Winning as a Modern Real Estate Agent*. Minneapolis, MN: RockPaperStar Press, 2016.

Turner, Mike. *Agent Entrepreneurs: Every Agent's Guide to What They Don't Teach You in Real Estate School*. Boise, ID: Fever Streak Press, 2016.

## WEBSITES

Because of the changing nature of internet links, Rosen Publishing has developed an online list of websites related to the subject of this book. This site is updated regularly. Please use this link to access the list:

http://www.rosenlinks.com/CCWC/shopping

# CHAPTER 6

# ANTIQUES DEALER

Perhaps you are one of those people who enjoys PBS's Antiques Roadshow. Every week, the show travels to a different city in the United States or Canada. At each stop, people are invited to bring in family heirlooms, garage sale finds, furnishings, ancient knickknacks, and decorative objects to be evaluated by antique specialists. The specialists discover the often fascinating histories of seemingly common or highly unusual objects and the astounding values they sometimes command. This is, in a nutshell, the job of an antiques dealer. If you love objects that have a history and think that tracking them down and purchasing them for resale would be an exciting challenge, antique dealing might be an ideal profession.

## WHAT THEY DO

An antiques dealer's job is to buy and sell antique objects and collector's items. They travel to auctions, flea and

Antiques dealers often frequent flea markets, looking for great deals on undervalued items. Once purchased and cleaned up and/or refurbished, the item can be sold at a higher price.

antique markets, trade fairs, estate and tag sales, and other dealers' shops, always on the lookout for interesting objects with artistic, historic, and monetary value. After purchasing any antiques, they then sell them to private clients, other dealers, or the public. As a dealer, you can sell your finds from an antique store (yours or another dealer's) or from a booth at an antique fair or market. You might even choose to work out of your home, inviting clients to visit you, and selling over the Internet.

Dealers often specialize in certain types of antiques. You may decide to focus on toys, silver, furniture, jewelry, books, or film posters. Then again, you may want to deal in objects from a specific era—the late 1800s or the 1920s, for example—or in items that are representative of a certain artistic style, such as baroque or art deco. To become a good dealer, you should begin by deciding what types of antiques really interest you and learning everything you can about them, including their histories and their potential values. Aside from having an eye for detail and a honed instinct for finding items, you'll have to spend a lot of time doing careful research. Reading and visiting museums, antique fairs, and other dealers will provide you with some essential background about antiques' histories and their values.

Antiques have no set prices. Their values can change based on factors ranging from condition (perfect or flawed) and rareness (one of a kind or unique) to importance as historical and artistic objects. Knowledge about such aspects is essential when you negotiate so that you get a good bargain when buying and make a profit when selling. Good salesmanship and a bit of charm can help you make a larger profit, which in turn will provide you with the capital to invest in more antiques of greater value.

A touch up of paint or varnish can take a damaged piece of furniture and turn it into something classic but brand-new.

In this way, your business will grow and you'll attract new customers. In the antique business, building up a large and loyal client base is key to survival. As you gain experience, you can also make money by advising owners on the value of their antiques for insurance or sales purposes. Aside from buying and selling antiques, some dealers work as appraisers for private clients or auction houses.

Traveling around in search of bargains and treasures can be exciting and bring you into contact with a lot of interesting people. However, it can also be expensive and entail a lot of hard work. It is very rare that one stumbles upon a precious object worth tens of thousands of dollars at a garage sale, but the dream of such a find is what inspires many buyers. Traveling, attending events and auctions, and meeting with clients means that antique dealers often work long hours, including evenings and weekends. Depending on the items in which you specialize, you also might have to do a fair amount of lifting and carrying. Used, faded, or damaged objects may need to be cleaned and restored before they can be resold. Some antique dealers end up doing some restoration work themselves.

## PREPARING FOR YOUR CAREER

Studying in art history is a great idea, but the best way to train for becoming an antiques dealer is the do-it-yourself method. This involves reading many books, specialized publications, and magazines as well as visiting museums, galleries, and antique stores and markets. Some museums and auction houses offer private training courses. However, the best education—and the most common way to get started professionally—is to get a job as an apprentice or assistant to an antique dealer. Working in a shop or at an auction house will provide constant exposure to different items as well as the art of pricing and negotiating. Since the field is fairly competitive, such jobs are not always easy to come by. However, once you get your foot in the door, it is easier to advance in the field. Ultimately, most jobs in the antique world aren't advertised, but they are announced via the professional grapevine. Once they have gained some experience and clients, many dealers decide to work on their own, gradually building up a collection of objects and a solid client base. You can begin by having a booth at antique fairs or markets or by selling out of your home, and eventually open your own business.

## JOB OUTLOOK AND SALARY

Salaries for those who work for a dealer or auction house are quite low because antiques dealers do the job because they love the work. Working for yourself, your income will depend on a combination of luck, talent, and skill at pricing and negotiating. Most profits you make will need to be invested in more antiques. On the positive side, antiques very rarely lose value. An average starting salary for an antique dealer is around $22,000 a year. After five years, this can increase significantly, and after ten to fifteen years, a dealer can make up to $61,000.

Although the antique business is highly competitive and requires a great deal of hard work, skill, and business savvy (as well as some luck), antiques will always be highly desired items. Unlike financial and art markets, which can fluctuate depending on outside circumstances, new trends, and fashions, antiques are always certain to rise in value. A more educated public that increasingly values unique design and fine craftsmanship of the past means that opportunities will continue to grow.

# FOR MORE INFORMATION

## ORGANIZATIONS

American Society of Appraisers
11107 Sunset Hills Road, Suite 310
Reston, VA 20190
(703) 478-2228
Website: http://www.appraisers.org/
The oldest major organization of professional
    appraisers. Members are experts in everything from
    carpets and cars to Asian and African art. The website
    includes links to publications and conferences.

Canadian Antique Dealers' Association
211 Cherry Hill Road
PO Box 81
Grafton, Ontario K0K 2G0
Canada
(416) 972-1378
Website: http://www.cadainfo.com/
This association regulates the purchasing of antiques
    in Canada. Its website offers news, links, and a list of
    shows and events.

Christie's
20 Rockefeller Plaza

New York, NY 10020

(212) 636-2000

Website: http://www.christies.com/

In existence since 1766, Christie's is one of the world's
major auction houses for antiques and art. The
website lists auctions and catalogs and offers virtual
tours as well as information for buyers, sellers, and
those seeking jobs.

National Antique & Art Dealers Association of America

220 E. 57th Street

New York, NY 10022

(212) 826-9707

Website: http://www.naadaa.org/

A nonprofit association that represents America's
leading art and antique dealers. NAADAA members
publish informative books and articles and organize
conferences about art and antiques for dealers and
the public.

Sotheby's

1334 York Avenue

New York, NY 10021

(212) 606-7000

Website: http://www.sothebys.com/
This renowned international auction house has been
   around since 1744. Sotheby's publishes books,
   catalogs, and provides information about auctions.

## BOOKS

Jordan, Wayne. *The Business of Antiques*. Fort Collins, CO:
   Krause Books, 2012.
Willard, Joe. *Picker's Bible: How to Pick Antiques Like the
   Pros*. Fort Collins, CO: Krause Books, 2014.

## WEBSITES

Because of the changing nature of internet links, Rosen
Publishing has developed an online list of websites
related to the subject of this book. This site is updated
regularly. Please use this link to access the list:

http://www.rosenlinks.com/CCWC/shopping

## CHAPTER 7

# ART DEALER/ GALLERY OWNER

Strolling through an art gallery, have you ever wished you could buy what you see hanging on the wall? Sound like a fantasy? Well, if you invest in a career as an art dealer, this fantasy could become reality. Although for you the fantasy might last only a short while, for your clients the pleasure of owning a unique, valuable, and beautiful work of art could last a lifetime.

## WHAT THEY DO

Art dealers purchase works of art so that they can sell them to other art lovers. Most art dealers own or work for galleries or have their

Art galleries are a bit like art museums, but the art is all for sale. Gallery owners tend to follow a particular art style, and buyers who like that type of art will often become regular clients.

own private offices where clients visit them. Their clients are generally fairly wealthy individuals interested in acquiring specific works for a private collection or as a financial investment. Sometimes, however, they simply want to decorate homes, offices, or other buildings with unique and beautiful art. Corporations and institutions such as cultural centers and museums also seek out art dealers, and many large companies collect, invest in, and exhibit art.

Based on your personal interests, as an art dealer you will specialize in certain artists or types of art (watercolor, sculpture, video art, Native American folk art), certain art schools or movements (the New York school, the impressionists), or the art of a certain period or region (eighteenth-century Dutch painting, early twentieth-century American photography). Specializing allows you to focus on a type of art that really interests you and distinguishes you from other dealers who are your competitors. It also narrows down the knowledge required for you to buy wisely and become a reputable dealer.

To be on top of what is going on in the art world, especially with respect to the type of art you buy, you'll constantly be visiting museums, galleries, auctions, and artists' studios as well as reading art journals and publications. You'll also have to be quite sociable, since networking with artists, museum curators, auction houses, and especially collectors and potential clients is an essential part of your job.

# DIFFERENT DEALERS

Let's take a look at some of the different types of art dealers.

Primary-market dealers discover new talent and help advance the careers of new artists by showing their works at galleries. This job includes meeting new people and visiting artists at work in their studios.

Second-market dealers handle works that have come on the market because of resale. If one of these dealers knows that a client—a private collector, museum, or other institution—is interested in such a work and it is within the dealer's area of expertise, he or she can negotiate its purchase.

Private dealers work in their own offices and meet with clients on an appointment-only basis. Private dealers can give more personalized attention to clients, educating them about works; visiting artists' studios, galleries, and art fairs with them; doing appraisals; and even attending auctions on their behalf.

Art consultants help inexperienced collectors make purchasing decisions by offering expert advice, taking them around to galleries, and helping them negotiate. Unlike dealers, consultants don't keep an inventory of artists' works. They earn commission (paid by the buyer, seller, or even both parties) whenever they succeed in negotiating a deal.

Ultimately, in the art world, most transactions depend on personal reputation and recommendations. In fact, much of your business—buying and selling—will often be carried out at exhibit openings and other social events. Once you build up a list of clients, you will spend your time seeking out particular works of art that they want for their collections.

Finding art to purchase can be a lot of fun and a great deal of work. You'll spend much of your time reading books, magazines, and sale catalogs from auction houses, as well as talking with art experts from other galleries and museums. You'll even have to stay alert for news of private collectors who have financial problems or have died; this could lead to the acquisition of an important piece of art. Once you find

Why should a client invest in a particular piece of art? Will the resale go up over time? Does the style work with his other belongings? Art dealers must know how to sell art to a client.

a piece that you or your client is interested in buying, you must be aware of its worth so that you don't pay too much or accept too little. Expert negotiating skills are crucial.

## PREPARING FOR YOUR CAREER

Now that you know what an art dealer does, it's time to talk about how to make that your career. Many dealers take courses or have college degrees in art history, but the surest route is probably on-the-job experience. In this competitive business, most people start out at the bottom, doing basic work—answering phones, doing research, and working in storage—as volunteers. Getting a job as an intern or an assistant at a gallery, museum, or auction house is a great way to start. You will learn about art and the business of buying and selling, and you will make contacts with artists and clients. Before opening their own galleries, many dealers work as curators in museums or auction houses, or as assistants at other people's galleries.

## JOB OUTLOOK AND SALARY

The majority of money that art dealers earn goes toward maintaining their gallery. What is left over is your "salary." The amount can vary enormously depending on the state of the art market, the health of the economy, and your ability to attract good artists and loyal clients. If you represent new artists, you'll often exhibit their work on consignment. When it is purchased, they will receive money while you receive a commission based on the sale. In other cases, you might be hired by a client to purchase a certain piece that isn't in your gallery, in which case you will receive a commission that might be between 7 and 10 percent of the work's price. In general, dealers who are starting out make around $30,000 a year. If you survive starting up and develop a good reputation, you can eventually earn $100,000 or even much more.

Art will always be a hot commodity, but the art market can be very unstable due to changing tastes, trends, and the economy. Even successful dealers can see their fortunes rise and fall over time. In 1990, for example, the art market crashed. Prices fell by 30 to 50 percent. In New York, a major art center, 70 of the city's 500 galleries went out of business. Nevertheless, established dealers with solid reputations can enjoy long, successful careers.

# FOR MORE INFORMATION

## ORGANIZATIONS

Art Dealers Association of America (ADAA)
205 Lexington Avenue, Suite 901
New York, NY 10016
(212) 488-5550
Website: http://www.artdealers.org/
This nonprofit organization of leading art dealers is a
good source for information about artists, galleries,
catalogs and publications (print and online),
collectors' resources, and appraisal services.

Art Dealers Association of Canada (ADAC)
401 Richmond Street West, Unit 393
Toronto, Ontario M5V 3A8
Canada
(416) 934-1583
Website: http://www.ad-ac.ca
The largest association of art galleries in Canada, whose
members represent the country's leading artists.
The ADAC offers information about Canadian and
international artists and dealers, markets, events,
publications, and employment opportunities.

National Antique & Art Dealers Association of America
  (NAADAA)
220 E. 57th Street
New York, NY 10022
(212) 826-9707
Website: http://www.naadaa.org/
A nonprofit association that represents America's
  leading art and antique dealers. NAADAA members
  publish informative books and articles and organize
  conferences about art and antiques for dealers and
  members of the public.

## BOOKS

Winkleman, Edward. *How to Start and Run a Commercial Art Gallery.* New York, NY: Allworth, 2010.

## WEBSITES

Because of the changing nature of internet links, Rosen Publishing has developed an online list of websites related to the subject of this book. This site is updated regularly. Please use this link to access the list:

http://www.rosenlinks.com/CCWC/shopping

# CHAPTER 8

# PURCHASING AGENT

The job of a purchasing agent is similar to that of a retail buyer. The main difference is that while retail buyers shop for products that will then be bought by the public, purchasing agents buy supplies for companies and manufacturers. If you like the wheeling and dealing of buying but not the stress of having to deal directly with changing consumer and marketing trends, you might want to consider a career as a purchasing agent.

## WHAT THEY DO

Purchasing agents track down everything businesses need to make goods or provide services. Factories, for example, depend upon purchasers to find quality materials at bargain prices so they can produce goods that are essential to the nation's economy. Many purchasing agents work in a specific industry, such as construction, electronics, communications, clothing, automobile, or metal or chemical fabrication.

Purchasing agents are in charge of ordering supplies and materials. They must keep track of current supplies and know when and how much of something to order.

Based on production schedules, they have to make sure that the right quantity of raw materials or supplies is being delivered to a manufacturer in order to keep production lines constantly moving. If you work in the clothing industry, for example, you'll be buying fabric, buttons, zippers, and other materials that are used to make clothes. If you work in the automobile industry, you'll be purchasing parts and materials—ranging from steel, tires, and spark plugs to engines and windows—used to assemble cars. Obviously, before you actually make a purchase, you'll have to know a considerable amount about the relevant supplies or materials.

Being a purchasing agent is a dynamic but high-pressure profession. If materials arrive damaged or late, or if you order too much or too little of an item, your company can lose money and credibility. If, however, you succeed in buying top-quality materials at rock-bottom prices and they arrive on time, you and your company can make a good profit.

Like retail buyers, purchasing agents must do an enormous amount of research before deciding what supplies to buy, in what quantity, and from whom. Talking with co-workers and studying your company's sales records, sales projections, and inventory levels will help you decide how much of what you need to buy. Reading industry publications and meeting with suppliers will help you decide with whom to do business. Getting together with suppliers often entails some traveling, sometimes even outside of the country. Being a good communicator and an excellent negotiator are key to cutting deals and signing purchasing contracts that will benefit your company.

Some purchasing agents also work for city, state, provincial, and federal governments. They are responsible for buying supplies and choosing service providers that are essential to the running of various government departments and agencies. For instance, you might need to contract a company to deliver office supplies, do construction work, or provide cleaning services for a government office building. You'll do this by reviewing bids and offers, often over the Internet, from various suppliers. Government purchasing agents have to follow strict rules when awarding contracts to avoid charges of favoritism.

Successful purchasing agents can be promoted to purchasing managers. Managers are in charge of supervising more complex buying operations as well as monitoring and training all agents and assistant or junior buyers. As a manager, you are ultimately responsible for all purchase decisions and the positive or negative effects they have on the company's fortunes.

## PREPARING FOR YOUR CAREER

Often, employers look for purchasing agents who have a college degree in business or economics. However, technical training or background in the industry in which you plan to work can also give you an edge. For example, knowing about computers and their parts can be a definite advantage if you want to become a purchasing agent for a computer manufacturer. Getting a part-time job or working as an intern to a purchaser can provide you with training and experience. Many companies have in-house training programs for purchasing agents where you can learn all about pricing, markets, and suppliers.

A good working knowledge of computers is important for the modern purchasing agent, as a good portion of ordering is done online.

Since the job market for purchasing agents and managers is competitive, it can help if you are professionally certified. The American Purchasing Society, the Institute for Supply Management, and the Purchasing Management Association of Canada offer certification based on education, work experience, and a written exam. Many government agencies require certification through the National Institute of Governmental Purchasing.

## JOB OUTLOOK AND SALARY

Purchasing agents are often well compensated for their efforts. On average, purchasing agents earn around $56,431 a year. Salaries for those starting out hover around $30,000, but those with more experience can eventually earn over $80,000. Purchasing managers earn an average yearly salary of $105,232 and, with time they can expect to earn over $120,000.

Jobs for purchasing agents and managers are not expected to increase in the future. Aside from a greater tendency to centralize buying decisions at a company's main headquarters, the main reason for this lack of growth is the increasing efficiency of technology. Computer software can track inventory, measure sales and stock levels, and automatically reorder supplies from manufacturers. Meanwhile, the Internet has simplified communication and research and allows contract bidding and purchases to be carried out electronically.

# FOR MORE INFORMATION

## ORGANIZATIONS

American Purchasing Society
P.O. Box 256
Aurora, IL 60507
(630) 859-0250
Website: http://www.american-purchasing.com
A national association of buyers and purchasing managers
that offers training, online courses, and recognized
certification programs for Certified Purchasing
Professional (CPP) and Certified Professional Purchasing
Manager (CPPM). The Website has information about
seminars, books, and finding jobs.

Federal Acquisition Institute (FAI)
9830 Belvoir Road, Building 270
Fort Belvoir, VA 22060
(703) 752-9604
Website: http://www.fai.gov/
FAI provides online courses, training, and other tools
to promote purchasing skills and knowledge. It
also publishes information on purchasing trends
and policies.

The Institute for Public Procurement
2411 Dulles Corner Park, Suite 350
Herndon, VA 20171
(800) FOR-NIGP or (703) 736-8900
Website: http://www.nigp.org
This nonprofit organization offers support to
     professionals in the public sector purchasing
     profession. NIGP provides services including
     education, professional networking, research,
     and technical assistance for purchasing agents
     throughout the United States and Canada.

Institute for Supply Management
2055 E. Centennial Circle
Tempe, AZ 85284
(800) 888-6276 or (480) 752-6276
Website: https://www.instituteforsupplymanagement.org
ISM provides education with respect to the purchasing
     and supply management profession.

## BOOKS

Monczka, Robert M., Robert B. Handfield, Larry C.
     Giunipero, and James L. Patterson. *Purchasing and*

*Supply Chain Management*. Chicago, IL: Cengage, 2015.

*Start Your Own Business*, 6th ed. Irvine, CA: Entrepreneur Press, 2015.

*Starting a Business All-in-One for Dummies*. Hoboken, NJ: Wiley, 2015.

## WEBSITES

Because of the changing nature of internet links, Rosen Publishing has developed an online list of websites related to the subject of this book. This site is updated regularly. Please use this link to access the list:

http://www.rosenlinks.com/CCWC/shopping

# CHAPTER 9

# STOCKBROKER/FINANCIAL ANALYST

Being a stockbroker is considered one of the most stressful jobs that exists. Buying company stock in order to earn money for clients is like getting paid to gamble. It can be exciting, not to mention extremely profitable, if you are a savvy and quick-thinking buyer. It can be disastrous if you aren't. If you love the idea of a career that is a roller coaster ride, with ups and downs but never a dull moment, you'd make a good candidate for a stockbroker.

## WHAT THEY DO

The job of a stockbroker is to buy stocks for individuals and corporations who have money to invest and want to make a profit. In order to buy or sell stock, people must go through a registered broker. A broker generally works for a financial institution, bank, or brokerage house that is a member of a stock exchange. You may have heard of major brokerage houses such as Merrill Lynch and Morgan Stanley. The

Stockbrokers need to be aware of stock values over the course of an entire day so that they can provide clients with the most up-to-date information. One mistake could lose a client a lot of money.

stock exchange is like a big market where stocks of public corporations are bought and sold by investors from all over the world.

If investors want to buy or sell stock, they will call you up and you'll get in touch with a trader who works on the floor of the stock exchange. After the trader buys or sells the stock, he will notify you, confirming that the

85

# HOW THE STOCK MARKET WORKS

We hear about the stock market on the news every day. However, most people don't really know how the stock market works. Here are some basic explanations:

When a person or a group of people want to start a business, they need capital (money). In order to raise capital, they create a public corporation. A corporation is an independent identity, a type of "virtual person" with its own social security number that can own property and in whose name deals and contracts can be signed.

After estimating how much their corporation needs, the owners issue shares. When investors—either individuals or companies—purchase shares, they are investing money in the company and becoming partial owners. The corporation can use this money to buy property, equipment, materials, and pay salaries, all with the aim of growing as a business and earning a profit.

Profits can be reinvested in the company to create more growth or paid out as dividends to shareholders. Ultimately, stock represents ownership of a company's assets and profits. Shareholders elect a board of directors to run the corporation efficiently and profitably.

Shares of stock are sold on stock exchanges. Canada's main stock exchange is the Toronto Stock Exchange (TSX), located on Bay Street. The three major stock exchanges in the United States are the American Stock Exchange (AMEX), the National Association of Securities Dealers Automated Quotations (NASDAQ), and the New York Stock Exchange (NYSE). The NYSE, located on Lower Manhattan's Wall Street, handles stock for close to 3,000 companies. Its total stock is worth more than 20 trillion dollars, making it the largest trading market in the world.

The New York Stock Exchange is located on Wall Street in New York City. It was established in 1792, with five securities being traded at that time. Today, the NYSE trades stocks for over 2,800 companies.

transaction was carried out according to regulations. After recording this information, you will inform your clients.

This process sounds simple, but it is actually quite complex. First of all, it takes years to build up a solid list of investor clients. To get clients, you have to be aggressive, confident, and good at networking. Even experienced brokers spend an enormous amount of time on the phone, trying to land new clients. You might end up making 100 calls a day! The way to get and keep clients is to impress them with your knowledge of the market. This requires staying up-to-date with everything that is going on in the domestic and global economy. You'll spend significant parts of your day reading economic papers, financial and industry reports, journals, and indexes; searching the Internet for new investment opportunities; and monitoring a client's current investments.

If stock prices are going to go up or down, you have to phone your client fast and together decide how much to buy or sell. This has to be done very quickly, since prices can rise and fall suddenly. Being responsible for your clients' investments—often their money is for children's college funds or their own retirement plans—is an enormous responsibility. Your timing and advice are crucial and can literally affect lives. Some brokers thrive in this exhilarating but stressful high-stakes atmosphere.

Others can't take it. Many new brokers leave within their first two years.

## PREPARING FOR YOUR CAREER

A college degree isn't necessary to become a stockbroker, but more stockbrokers are attending college. As markets and economies grow more complex, studying subjects such as business, economics, and finance can help give you a solid background. Since more and more stock market transactions are being done by computer, some computer background is also useful. Probably the best training you can get, however, is on-the-job experience. In the end, knowing how to instill confidence in customers is the most important skill for a successful broker.

When you first start out working for a brokerage firm, you will receive in-house training. This may last anywhere from four months to two years. Since all brokers need to be registered, most firms will also help you prepare for the General Securities Registered Representative Exam, administered by the National Association of Securities Dealers (NASD). Depending on your state of residence, you may also need to pass the Uniform Securities Agents State Law Examination that gives you a license to be a stockbroker. In Canada, registration and qualification are monitored by the Investment Dealers Association of Canada (IDA).

## JOB OUTLOOK AND SALARY

When you start out as a broker, before you have any clients of your own, you will probably receive a small base salary from the firm that hired you. However, once you start establishing your own list of clients, you will also start earning commission. Commission is a percentage of the value of your client's transactions. This means that the more clients you have, and the more you can convince them to buy or sell, the more commission you will make. Because of this, most brokers are psyched to sell—their efforts can literally make them millionaires.

In truth, however, very few brokers become millionaires. The average American broker earns a comfortable $71,720 a year. But those Wall Street and Bay Street players who have a knack for working hard and selling hard can easily earn between $100,000 and $150,000; sometimes they earn much more. Of course, earnings depend enormously on the state of the economy and the market. During rough times, even top brokers can see their commissions disappear as investors stop buying.

As people's incomes increase, they will seek more investment opportunities. There will be particular growth with respect to individuals making their own investments for their retirement. Also, as the market becomes increasingly global, new opportunities will open up. At the same time, however, as buying and selling stocks over the Internet becomes more common, brokers can take on more clients, making it tougher for newcomers breaking into the field.

Beginning brokers always have a tough time. Starting out, without a client list, can be difficult and very competitive. Competition is especially intense in large firms, particularly those in New York, where there are often more applicants than jobs.

# FOR MORE INFORMATION

## ORGANIZATIONS

The Canadian Securities Administrators (CSA)
Tour de la Bourse
800 Square Victoria, Suite 2510
Montreal, QC H4Z 1J2
Canada
(514) 864-9510
Website: http://www.csa-acvm.ca/
The CSA coordinates regulation of the Canadian capital
markets with the aim of protecting market investors
from improper practices.

Securities Industry and Financial Markets Association
120 Broadway, 35th Floor
New York, NY 10271
(212) 313-1200
Website: http://www.sifma.org
An association of investment bankers, brokers, dealers,
and mutual fund companies concerned with building
public trust and confidence in trading markets. Offers
training and education for members, and information
and services to the public.

U.S. Securities and Exchange Commission (SEC)
SEC Headquarters

100 F Street, NE
Washington, DC 20549
(202) 942-8088
Website: http://www.sec.gov/
The SEC protects investors against misinformation
and fraud. It makes and enforces laws and rules that
govern the securities industry in the United States to
ensure investors receive all the information they need
to make sound investments.

## BOOKS

Griffis, Michael and Lita Epstein. *Trading for Dummies*.
Hoboken, NJ: Wiley, 2013.

## WEBSITES

Because of the changing nature of internet links, Rosen
Publishing has developed an online list of websites
related to the subject of this book. This site is updated
regularly. Please use this link to access the list:

http://www.rosenlinks.com/CCWC/shopping

# CHAPTER 10

## SECRET SHOPPER

Have you ever envisioned a job that would allow you to spend your days buying clothes, seeing movies, working out at health clubs, and eating in popular restaurants? The thought is appealing, isn't it? Now imagine getting paid to do all these things. It might sound like a fantasy or a put-on, but thousands of people across North America are supplementing their incomes and even making a living by going shopping. Because they do so undercover, they are known as secret shoppers.

A secret shopper's job is to keep an eye on the day-to-day operations of a restaurant or retail store. Secret shoppers follow a specific plan and then report back report back to their hiring agency.

## WHAT THEY DO

You've likely heard the saying "The customer is always right." Unfortunately, not all businesses can be sure that their clients are always treated the way they deserve. Sometimes customers in stores, restaurants, or theaters are treated quite poorly. Marketing surveys have found that while customers who are well served share their positive experiences with three other people, those who are ignored, insulted, or irritated will complain to at least ten people. Faced with rising competition, businesses that provide services can't afford to lose customers. Increasingly, they are hiring secret shoppers to make sure that their establishments and employees are working to make clients feel like royalty.

## ALIAS

Secret shoppers are known by a variety of names...

auditors
consumer researchers
customer service researchers
market researchers
mystery shoppers
scouts
service evaluators

Working undercover, secret shoppers are a company's eyes and ears. They provide detailed impressions from a shopper's point of view. Most secret shoppers get jobs from secret shopping companies. These firms have a variety of clients, ranging from supermarkets and chain clothing stores to movie theaters and amusement parks.

When you receive an assignment to have lunch at a restaurant, get your hair done at a salon, or buy toys for your (real or imaginary) toddler, it will generally be in your town and even in your neighborhood. Often, you choose the day and even the time you want to go

How quickly does it take an employee to wait on you at a retail clothing store? Is the order you receive in a restaurant exactly as it was listed on the menu? It's a secret shopper's job to find out.

shopping. Expenses such as transportation are usually reimbursed.

As a secret shopper, you have to act like any other shopper. The difference is that you will be observing every detail of the business you are visiting, albeit very discreetly. You'll also need to take notes in your head, with a pen and paper, or even with a camera (this is known as enhanced shopping). Among your goals is to observe whether employees are doing their jobs efficiently and treating customers well. Are salespeople friendly and knowledgeable about the products they are selling? Do cashiers give proper change and receipts? You'll also determine whether the business in question meets with all safety, security, and hygienic standards. Are bathrooms clean and stocked with toilet paper? Is the lighting bright enough? Is produce old or damaged? Is the fire escape blocked? Was that a cockroach running across the floor? Not only will your observations help businesses improve their services, but they can also alert owners to serious problems that could otherwise result in accidents, expensive fines, and damaging lawsuits.

Sometimes, secret shoppers actually make purchases. While you usually can't keep the clothes, you can eat the food at a restaurant, sample the rides at an amusement park, and watch the movie at a theater (often with

## WHAT DO SECRET SHOPPERS DO?

Car dealers and rental companies
Banks
Convenience stores and supermarkets
Gas stations
Department stores and clothing chains
Movie theaters and amusement parks
Hotels and motels
Restaurants
Hair salons
Health clubs
Government-run businesses and services

popcorn). Other times, however, you simply evaluate a service. Some people are even hired to do online shopping by visiting eebsites. Once your shopping session is over, you have to fill out a detailed form with your observations. Being a clear and precise writer is important. Although secret shoppers are usually hired to give a company feedback on its own products and services, in some cases you'll be hired to shop a business's main competition.

## PREPARING FOR YOUR CAREER

There is no training required to become a secret shopper. However, there are various seminars and workshops you can take. You can consult guide books for tips on breaking into the business and lists of the most reputable secret shopping companies. The National Center for Professional Mystery Shoppers & Merchandisers is a good source for information. This organization offers the KASST (Knowledge and Skill Set Test), an exam that allows you to call yourself a certified mystery shopper.

## JOB OUTLOOK AND SALARY

Payment is contingent upon the type of shopping you do and the number of hours you work. Sometimes, you'll also receive an allowance for purchases and a reimbursement for your expenses. If you're working under contract for a mystery shopping company, you can expect to earn about $100 a month in cash, food, and merchandise if you shop once a week (an average of two to four hours of work in a month). If you become contracted by more companies, you can shop and earn much more. Many secret shoppers, particularly students, homemakers, and retired people, are content to work part-time. However, if you are ambitious, organized, and succeed in getting yourself contracted by ten or twenty top mystery-shopping companies (there are hundreds of companies, but some are hoaxes) you can earn as much as $40,000 a year. You might even want to consider opening up your own mystery shopping company with your own list of clients and team of mystery shoppers.

Secret shopping is a fairly new business. Since companies can't send the same people to shop at the same places, mystery shopping companies are in constant need of new shoppers.

# FOR MORE INFORMATION

## ORGANIZATIONS

MSPA Americas
12300 Ford Road, Suite 135
Dallas, TX 75234
(972) 406-1104
Website: http://www.mspa-na.org
The MSPA is a worldwide professional trade association
dedicated to improving service quality by using
anonymous shoppers.

National Shopping Service
2510 Warren Drive, Suite B
Rocklin, CA 95677
(800) 800-2704
Website: http://www.nationalshoppingservice.com/
After thirty-three successful years, NSS has developed
into one of the world's leading mystery shopping
providers. Register and begin your career as a mystery
shopper.

Secret Shopper
620 Mendelssohn Ave N
Minneapolis, MN 55427-4310
(763) 525-1460

Website: https://www.secretshopper.com
Secret Shopper® has delivered actionable market
 research and analysis to our clients for over 25 years.

## BOOKS

Mooradian, Bethany. *The Mystery Shopper Training
 Program*. Seattle, WA: Amazon Digital Services, 2015.
Wilson, Brad. *Do More, Spend Less: The New Secrets of
 Living the Good Life for Less*. Hoboken, NJ: Wiley, 2013.

## WEBSITES

Because of the changing nature of internet links, Rosen
Publishing has developed an online list of websites
related to the subject of this book. This site is updated
regularly. Please use this link to access the list:

http://www.rosenlinks.com/CCWC/shopping

# CHAPTER 11

# WINE MERCHANT/ BUYER

Imagine a job that allows you to travel around the world, visit vineyards, and taste the most delicious, sometimes rarest, wines on the planet. This is how wine merchants spend much of their time. Of course, after purchasing the best of what they've tasted, they have to return home and consider how to make money by sharing their discoveries with people who frequent their shops, stores, and restaurants.

## WHAT THEY DO

A wine merchant or buyer is an expert at purchasing wines. You can learn about wine by reading

The grapes that are used to make wine are different from the grapes you buy at the store to eat. There are thousands of different types of wine grapes.

books and magazines, but there is no substitute for using your senses. Learning to judge a wine by its scent and, more importantly, its taste are key skills. Most wine merchants develop these skills by going to organized wine tastings and traveling to the vineyards where the wines are produced.

Discovering wine from a new region can be just as exciting as savoring a centuries-old classic vintage. Visiting producers allows you to see firsthand all the factors that go into making a good wine, from soil and sunlight to harvest and storage techniques. It is also essential to forge good personal relationships with vintners so you can negotiate pricing and shipping details and monitor production standards (the use of high quality grapes and proper storage methods, for example).

Many wine merchants are also wine retailers who own or run their own specialty wine shops. Through foreign producers and distributors, local importers and wholesalers, and the Internet, merchants shop for an assortment of wines that will please their customers. In North America, people are increasingly interested in wine and are drinking it more frequently. Although consumers like to try new wines, those who aren't collectors or connoisseurs often don't know which wines to select. Part of your job as a merchant is to stock a wide variety of wines for different tastes and budgets and to educate your clients as to what choices are available.

# THE LIFE OF A WINE MERCHANT

David Andrew is from Scotland, where men drink mostly whiskey, not wine. However, when he was ten, his parents let him have his first taste of wine and he was smitten. More than twenty years later, Andrew has worked his way up to top wine buyer for America's warehouse supermarket giant Costco.

Surprising as it might seem, Costco is actually the largest wine retailer in North America, with annual sales of $600 million in 2002. And its high revenues aren't due to selling bottles of wine for $3.99 apiece. Thanks to Andrew's smart purchasing practices, Costco's clients can pick up anything from a delicious $10 bottle of Chilean red wine to a precious 1998 bottle of Chateau Mouton Rothschild for $165. In fact, an important part of Andrew's job is to journey all over the world seeking out bargains and undiscovered treasures. An example is a Chateau Salitis, a French red known as a boutique wine because only 5,000 cases are made each year (Andrew buys almost all of them for Costco). During his travels, he is wined and dined by vintners and ends up tasting over 5,000 wines. If this seems like an awful lot to drink, remember that to keep their tasting abilities sharp and to avoid getting tipsy, professional tasters spit out instead of swallowing.

Advising customers on what wines are suitable for certain types of meals or events is another important task.

As wine sales have increased across North America, wine has moved onto the shelves of larger retailers. People who buy wines on a large scale for liquor stores, supermarkets, wholesalers, and importers are often referred to as wine buyers or wine managers. Wine buyers have to make sure shelves are always filled with wines that are going to sell well. Aside from researching new wines, placing orders with suppliers, and monitoring transportation and delivery, wine buyers organize promotions and displays and create marketing materials to educate both workers and customers.

Wine merchants have to know what they're selling. Wine quality is determined by the wine's scent and taste, including intensity, complexity, and balance.

Wine buyers are also employed by airlines, cruise ships, and hotels. Upscale hotels and restaurants with extensive wine cellars often employ a sommelier as well. A sommelier is a wine steward. Sommeliers help create a wine menu based on costs, clientele, and a restaurant's cuisine. Aside from selecting and purchasing wines, sommeliers must train staff to treat wine properly (how to open and serve it, for example), and make appropriate suggestions to customers based on the food they are eating and the money they are willing to spend. A knowledgeable sommelier can make a big difference in a restaurant's profits since aperitifs, wine, and an after-dinner port or sherry might represent 20 to 40 percent of a customer's lunch or dinner check.

## PREPARING FOR YOUR CAREER

You do not have to have a formal education to work as a wine merchant. The best thing to do is learn all you can about wine. Many books, magazines, journals, and websites are available. Continuing education, hotel and restaurant schools, and culinary institutes offer courses on various aspects of wine tasting and selection. Find out about wine tastings organized by local vinyard, wine societies, restaurants, or specialty shops. And if you can swing it, travel to a wine producing region and learn firsthand about wine by meeting vintners and sampling their wares. Any kind of part-time or summer job in the wine industry will help you learn about wine and retail and provide you with useful contacts. Working at a vineyard, or wine shop, or as a waiter or bartender's assistant in a hotel or restaurant are all excellent ways to learn about the business.

## JOB OUTLOOK AND SALARY

Salaries for wine merchants vary, based on whether you have your own store or work as a buyer for a large retail chain. Starting out you might earn only $29,000 a year. If you are successful and work your way up to a top buyer or managerial position, you could earn as much as $90,000.

Job opportunities in the wine industry are expected to increase as North Americans become more educated about wines, realize the health benefits, and have increased access to wines from all over the world.

# FOR MORE INFORMATION

## ORGANIZATIONS

American Sommelier
Bowling Green Station
PO Box 590
New York, NY 10274
(212) 226-6805
Website: http://www.americansommelier.com/
A nonprofit, national organization uniting local
   chapters that run classes, meetings, tastings, and
   events that revolve around wine education and
   enjoyment. Also offers courses and certification for
   sommeliers.

Wine Institute
425 Market Street, Suite 1000
San Francisco, CA 94105
(415) 356-7569
Website: http://www.wineinstitute.org
Wine Institute is the voice for California wine
   representing more than 1,000 wineries and
   affiliated businesses from the beautiful and diverse
   wine regions throughout the state.

## BOOKS

Bastianich, Joseph and David Lynch. *Vino Italiano: The Regional Wines of Italy*. New York, NY: Clarkson Potter, 2012.

## PERIODICALS

Food and Wine
American Express Publishing Corp.
1120 Avenue of the Americas
New York, NY 10036
A glossy print magazine that marries gourmet food recipes with fine wine offerings. Articles on cooking, entertaining, and dining out, as well as reviews of food, wine shops, and kitchen equipment.

## WEBSITES

Because of the changing nature of internet links, Rosen Publishing has developed an online list of websites related to the subject of this book. This site is updated regularly. Please use this link to access the list:

http://www.rosenlinks.com/CCWC/shopping

# CHAPTER 12

# FASHION CONSULTANT

When you pick up a magazine or visit your favorite fashion blogs, you'll often see photos of celebrities immaculately dressed. Famous people have to look good on the red carpet, but did you know that many pay experts to tell them what to wear to the supermarket? In a media culture, where image is everything (and best- and worst-dressed lists are everywhere), most high-profile people who spend time in the public eye no longer dare to dress themselves. Instead they rely on the expert advice and resources of fashion consultants or wardrobe stylists.

## WHAT THEY DO

If you have an instinctive talent for finding the perfect dress, suit, tie, earrings, handbag, or pair of sunglasses that will make heads turn and flashbulbs go off, being a fashion consultant might be the perfect job for you. Most celebrities, particularly Hollywood stars, can't make it through the week without consulting their stylists. However, wardrobe stylists also work to find ideal clothing and accessories for men, women, children, and even

Fashion consultants can recommend the right outfit for almost anyone, within any budget. They shop in-person and online to find the best deals.

animals that are going to appear in films, videos, television programs, commercials, theatrical and musical productions, fashion layouts, and magazine spreads. This job can be a creative challenge if you're working on an eighteenth-century French costume drama, a revival of Grease, or a science fiction thriller set in the year 3000.

To be a successful stylist, you need a good sense of style and the ability to visualize what kinds of clothing work for a certain person in a specific setting. Attention to detail is important. So is staying up to date with new trends and fashions and knowing what kind of style will appeal to a particular audience.

The majority of stylists work as freelancers. They are hired by photographers; stage, film, or video directors; or art directors for magazines, catalogs, and advertising firms. Your work as a stylist will usually consist of short-term projects. Hours tend to be long, deadlines are tight, and the work atmosphere is creative but stressful. If you have a large wardrobe budget at your disposal, you can have a lot of fun shopping for major designer labels. More often than not, however, small budgets will force you to look for creative solutions. Good business sense and knowing how to manage your time and finances are essential skills.

After hunting down and purchasing the clothes and accessories required, you will be in charge of caring for them and deciding how they will be worn by actors, models, or other clients. As part of an artistic team, you'll have to deal sensitively with the director's ego as well as those of the people wearing the clothes. Stories of clients who refuse to wear a certain suit or gown at the last minute, causing a stylist to seek frantically for an alternate solution, are common. A well-known Hollywood wardrobe stylist once claimed that her favorite actor was a chimpanzee because he didn't talk back to her or drop his clothes all over the floor.

Most stylists get jobs by building up an impressive body of work and a good reputation. A lot of jobs come from word-of-mouth recommendations. It is also important to have a portfolio with samples of your work—either

# FASHION CONSULTANTS ON THE JOB

Jami's actress friends were the first ones to suggest she become a fashion consultant. Jami herself had never even heard of that career path. A clothes-lover with her own unique style, she volunteered as an apprentice for a well-known stylist, which involved carrying around a lot of heavy shopping bags. Among the insider tips she learned was where to find the best military uniforms and evening wear, what tailors could do overnight alterations, and where she could find clothing for dogs.

In her fourteen-year career, Jami has often come to the rescue in fashion emergencies. One involved an actress who tried to glue in her hair extensions using Krazy Glue. She wound up with her lips glued together and her shirt glued to her chest. Another time—in the days before silicone—Jami had to quickly create a pair of fake breasts out of shoulder pads and duct tape.

photographs or videos—and a resumé that includes important projects and clients. Many professional stylists have their own agents who book jobs for them and manage their contracts. Some travel is usually entailed as you shuttle from stores and tailors to private homes, studios, theaters, or film sets.

## PREPARING FOR YOUR CAREER

Most fashion consultants have some experience in art or fashion. Aside from staying tuned to new trends, it helps to take some courses in art, fashion, or photography at community colleges or as part of a continuing education program. You can learn tricks of the trade and make contacts by apprenticing with a professional stylist. Volunteering your services—usually running errands— might eventually lead to a position as a paid assistant. Stylists who work on major film, television, and theater productions often have to be members of the International Alliance of Theatrical Stage Employees, Moving Picture Technicians, Artists and Allied Crafts (IATSE).

## JOB OUTLOOK AND SALARY

Salaries vary for fashion consultants. Depending on their reputations and client lists, stylists working in the two major markets of New York City and Los Angeles can earn anywhere from $300 to $900 a day. Assistants earn between $150 and $200. This might seem like a lot of money, but many stylists have to deduct health insurance as well as fees paid to agents who get them their jobs. Only top stylists get enough work to keep them constantly busy. Although a few stylists have permanent, full-time jobs, many freelancers go weeks without work. Outside of New York and Los Angeles, fees are lower and work is hard to come by. Aside from consulting with private clients, many stylists also work as make-up artists or hair stylists.

Fashion is fluid, constantly changing. And your individual tastes within fashion are extremely important. Your personal style will help determine what you might recommend to a client.

The fact that North Americans on the whole are increasingly style-conscious means that people will be willing to spend more money on stylists. In the last fifteen years, stylists have gone from being seen as mere "frock finders" to style gurus who are sought out by celebrities as well as designers who want to promote their clothes and accessories. However, even as stylists become more important, the field is incredibly competitive and remains largely centered in major cities such as New York; Los Angeles; and Toronto, Canada.

# FOR MORE INFORMATION

## ORGANIZATIONS

The International Alliance of Theatrical Stage
  Employees, Moving Picture Technicians, Artists and
  Allied Crafts of the United States, Its Territories and
  Canada (IATSE)
207 W. 25th St., 4th floor
New York, NY 10001
(212) 730-1770
Website: http://www.iatse.net
The IATSE is the main labor union representing
  technicians and craftspeople in the entertainment
  industry, including theater, film, and
  television production.

## PERIODICALS

Elle
300 West 57th Street, 24th floor
New York, NY 10019
Website: http://www.elle.com/
Leading fashion magazine for young women with lively,
  down-to-earth features on beauty, style, shopping,
  and runway fashions.

Harper's BAZAAR
300 West 57th Street
New York, NY 10019
(212) 903-5000
Website: http://www.harpersbazaar.com/
A style bible with notes and news on latest trends and
   fashions, as well as tips for where to shop for them.
   The fashion editorials are produced by some of the
   world's leading photographers.

Vogue
Condé Nast Publications
1 World Trade Center
New York, NY 10048
Website: http://www.vogue.com
A legendary women's fashion magazine with the world's
   most elegant and sophisticated clothing and jewelry
   featured in its glossy pages.


W
Condé Nast Publications
1 World Trade Center
New York, NY 10048

Website: http://www.wmagazine.com
An oversized fashion and lifestyle magazine with
   in-depth articles about the international fashion
   scene accompanied by glamorous photos by the
   globe's top fashion photographers.

## WEBSITES

Because of the changing nature of internet links, Rosen
Publishing has developed an online list of websites
related to the subject of this book. This site is updated
regularly. Please use this link to access the list:

http://www.rosenlinks.com/CCWC/shopping

# GLOSSARY

**COMMISSION** A fee or percentage of proceeds paid to a broker or agent for his or her services.

**COMMODITY** A product that is bought and resold.

**CONSIGNMENT** A form of buying in which the dealer pays the owner after the goods have been sold.

**CONTRACTOR** A person who agrees to supply certain materials or do certain work, usually for a predetermined sum.

**DISCREETLY** With restraint or care.

**ENHANCE** To improve in cost, value, or attractiveness.

**FLAIR** A natural talent or ability.

**FRANCHISE** An agreement in which a company allows another party to use its brand name and to sell or rent its products or services.

**GURU** A trusted guide or advisor.

**LAYOUT** The overall design of a page, spread, or book.

**MEDIATOR** Someone who works to reach an agreement between people or parties.

**PORTFOLIO** A flat, portable case for holding material, such as photographs or drawings.

**SURPLUS** A quantity or amount in excess of what is needed.

**WHOLESALER** A person or firm that sells goods in large quantities and usually at lower prices than retail.

# BIBLIOGRAPHY

Fireman, Judy. "A Day in the Life of an Independent Professional: A Winning Proposition" 1099 Magazine, September 14, 1999. Retrieved July 2005. http://www .1099.com/c/ar/di/props_d011.html.

Fonda, Daren. "Chateau Margaux Meets Costco." *Time*, October 20, 2002. Retrieved July 2005. http://www.time .com/time/globalbusiness/article/0,9171,1101021028 -366290,00.html.

Ginsberg, Merle. "Dressing to Thrill: Wardrobe Stylist Sought by International Fashion Designers." *Los Angeles* magazine, September 1998. Retrieved July 1998. http:// www.findarticles.com/p/articles/mi_m1346/is_n9_v43 /ai_21029536/pg_1.

Obringer, Lee Ann. "How Buying a House Works." HowStuffWorks. Retrieved June 2005. http://money .howstuffworks.com/house-buying.htm.

Sheppard, Lauren. "Dream Job: Hollywood Wardrobe Stylist." Salary.com. Retrieved July 2005. http://www.salary.com /careers/layoutscripts/crel_display.asp?tab=cre&cat =Cat10&ser=Ser71&part=Par157.

# INDEX

## ABOUT THE AUTHOR

Edson Santos grew up in Rio de Janeiro and Miami. While acquiring a bachelor's degree in literature from New York University, Edson supported himself with many buying-related jobs, some of which—such as secret shopper, professional shopper, and broker (he was a part-time receptionist at a Wall Street brokerage firm)—are listed in this book.

Rebecca Pelos is a nonfiction writer with experience in job hunting and career guidance. She lives in Tennessee.

## PHOTO CREDITS

Cover, p. 1 Dragon Images/Shutterstock.com; pp. 4–5 Rawpixel.com/Shutterstock.com; p. 8 g-stockstudio/Shutterstock.com; p. 12 Maksym Poriechkin/Shutterstock.com; pp. 16–17 Monkey Business Images/Shutterstock.com; p. 22 mavo/Shutterstock.com; pp. 26–27 © iStockphoto.com/SolStock; p. 29 lightpoet/Shutterstock.com; p. 38 © iStockphoto.com/AscentXmedia; p. 41 bikeriderlondon/Shutterstock.com; p. 48 © iStockphoto.com/Martin Dimitrov; p. 50 © iStockphoto.com/kokouu; p. 57 Radiokafka/Shutterstock.com; p. 59 © iStockphoto.com/cometary; pp. 66–67 © iStockphoto.com/Willie B. Thomas; p. 70 © iStockphoto.com/TommL; p. 76 © iStockphoto.com/Juanmonino; p. 79 © iStockphoto.com/Xavier Arnau; p. 85 © iStockphoto.com/Rawpixel Ltd; p. 87 Stuart Monk/Shutterstock.com; pp. 94–95 Peter Bernik/Shutterstock.com; p. 97 Olesia Bilkei/Shutterstock.com; pp. 104–105 mythja/Shutterstock.com; p. 108 Mintybear/Shutterstock.com; pp. 114–115 © iStockphoto.com/funstock; pp. 118–119 © iStockphoto.com/PeopleImages; cover and interior design elements © iStockphoto.com/David Shultz (dots), Melamory/Shutterstock.com (hexagon pattern), Lost & Taken (boxed text background texture), snorks/Shutterstock.com (chapter opener pages icons).

Designer: Brian Garvey; Editor: Bethany Bryan; Photo researcher: Karen Huang